696 SILLY
SCHOOL JOKES & RIDDLES

by **JOSEPH ROSENBLOOM**

illustrated by
Dennis Kendrick

 Sterling Publishing Co., Inc.   New York

To Brett Backerman

Library of Congress Cataloging-in-Publication Data

Rosenbloom, Joseph.
  696 silly school jokes & riddles.

  Includes index.
  Summary: A collection of 696 jokes, riddles, and
tongue twisters on the subject of school.
  1. Education—Juvenile humor. 2. Wit and humor,
Juvenile. [1. Schools—Wit and humor. 2. Jokes.
3. Riddles. 4. Tongue twisters] I. Kendrick, Dennis,
ill. II. Title. III. Title: Six hundred ninety-six
silly school jokes and riddles.
PN6231.S3R67 1986   818′.5402   85-27855
ISBN 0-8069-4726-8
ISBN 0-8069-4727-6 (lib. bdg.)

ISBN 0-8069-6392-1 (paper)

Contents

Books by Joseph Rosenbloom

Biggest Riddle Book in the World
Daffy Definitions
Doctor Knock-Knock's Official Knock-Knock
  Dictionary
Funniest Joke Book Ever!
Funniest Riddle Book Ever!
Funny Insults & Snappy Put-Downs
Gigantic Joke Book
Knock-Knock Who's There
Looniest Limerick Book in the World
Mad Scientist
Monster Madness
Nutty Knock Knocks
Official Wild West Joke Book
Ridiculous Nicholas Haunted House Riddles
Ridiculous Nicholas Pet Riddles
Ridiculous Nicholas Riddle Book
Silly Verse (and Even Worse)
Wacky Insults and Terrible Jokes
Zaniest Riddle Book in the World

1. FIRST THINGS FIRST

What is the first thing a little snake learns in school?
Hiss-tory.

What is the first thing a little gorilla learns in school?
The Ape B C's.

What do little astronauts get when they do their homework?
Gold stars.

Why did the little vampires stay up all night?
They were studying for a blood test.

TEACHER: Alice, name four members of the cat family.
ALICE: Mother, father, sister and brother.

TEACHER: Pablo, name six wild animals.
PABLO: Two lions and four tigers.

5

WHY DID THEY DO WELL IN SCHOOL?

—The firefly?
It was so bright.

—The duck?
It was a wise quacker.

—The two-headed monster?
Two heads are better than one.

—The elephant?
It had a lot of grey matter.

—The balloon?
It went to the top of the class.

TEACHER: How old were you on your last birthday?
STUDENT: Seven.
TEACHER: How old will you be on your next birthday?
STUDENT: Nine.
TEACHER: That's impossible.
STUDENT: No, it isn't, teacher. I'm eight today.

WHY DID THEY FLUNK OUT?

—The little witches?
They couldn't spell.

—The skeleton?
His heart wasn't in it.

—The owl?
It didn't give a hoot.

Where do monsters study?
In ghoul school.

Who sits in front of the class in ghoul school?
The creature teacher.

"Teacher, may I leave the room?"
  "Well, you certainly can't take it with you."

TEACHER: George, go to the map and find North
  America.
GEORGE: Here it is!
TEACHER: Correct. Now, class, who discovered
  America?
CLASS: George!

Where do you find prehistoric cows?
  In a moo-seum.

TEACHER: Willy, name one important thing we have
  today that we didn't have ten years ago.
WILLY: Me!

FIRST DAY OF SCHOOL

Sally came home from her first day at school.

"It was all right," she told her mother, "except for some lady named Teacher who kept spoiling our fun."

Larry came home from his first day at school.

"I'm not going back," he said.

"Why not?" asked his father.

"Because my teacher doesn't know anything," said Larry. "All she ever does is ask questions."

Elroy came home from his first day at school.

"Nothing much happened," he told his mother. "Some lady didn't know how to spell 'cat.' I told her."

TEACHER: Do you know "London Bridge Is Falling Down?"

SARA: No, but I hope no one gets hurt.

SUZIE: I won a prize in kindergarten today. The teacher asked me how many legs a hippopotamus had. I said three.

FATHER: Three? How on earth did you win the prize?

SUZIE: I came the closest.

PRINCIPAL: What are you going to be when you get out of school?

HARVEY: An old man.

Marvin came into his kindergarten class with a squirming worm.

"What are you doing with that disgusting worm?" asked his teacher.

"We were playing outside," said Harvey, "and I thought I'd show him my kindergarten."

TEACHER SAYS

Say each sentence three times quickly:

• Rubber buggy bumpers.

• Bobby Blue blows big blue bubbles.

• The big beautiful blue balloon burst.

How does a skeleton study for tests?
It bones up.

With tears in his eyes, the little boy told his kindergarten teacher that only one pair of boots was left in the classroom and they weren't his.

The teacher searched and searched, but she couldn't find any other boots. "Are you sure these boots aren't yours?" she asked.

"I'm sure," the little boy sobbed. "Mine had snow on them."

TEACHER: Why do traffic lights turn red?
DOLLY: You would too if you had to stop and go in the middle of the street.

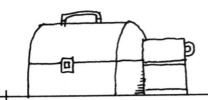

WHAT DID YOU LEARN IN SCHOOL TODAY?

MOTHER: What did you learn in school today?

AUDREY: Not enough. I have to go back tomorrow.

MOTHER: What did you learn in school today?

LOUELLA: How to talk without moving my lips.

FATHER: What did you learn in school today?

LOUIE: My teacher taught us how to write.

FATHER: What did you write?

LOUIE: I don't know, Dad. She didn't teach us how to read yet.

TEACHER: Goodness, Mildred, haven't you finished washing that blackboard yet? You've been at it for an hour.

MILDRED: I know, but the more I wash it, the blacker it gets.

WATSON: What school did you go to, Holmes?
SHERLOCK: Elementary, my dear Watson!

It was the first day of school. As the principal made his rounds, he heard a terrible commotion coming from one of the classrooms. He rushed in and spotted one boy, taller than the others, who seemed to be making the most noise. He seized the lad, dragged him into the hall, and told him to wait there until he was excused.

Returning to the classroom, the principal restored order and lectured the class for half an hour about the importance of good behavior.

"Now," he said, "are there any questions?"

One girl stood up timidly. "Please, sir," she asked, "may we have our teacher back?"

SUBSTITUTE TEACHER: Are you chewing gum?
BILLY: No, I'm Billy Anderson.

What is big and yellow and comes in the morning to brighten Mother's day?
The school bus.

Mrs. Jones brought her son Elmer to register at school. However, Elmer was only five, and the required age was six.

"I think," said Mrs. Jones to the principal, "that he can pass the six-year-old test."

"We'll see," replied the principal. "Elmer, say the first thing that comes to your mind."

"Do you want logically connected sentences," said Elmer, "or purely irrelevant words?"

What's one and one?
Two.
What's four minus two?
Two.
Who wrote Tom Sawyer?
Twain.
Now say all the answers together.
Two, two, twain.
Have a nice twip!

2. HOME ROOM HI-JINKS

TEACHER: Alfred, how can one person make so many stupid mistakes in one day?
ALFRED: I get up early.

GRACE: What time do you wake up in the morning?
ACE: About an hour and a half after I get to school.

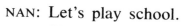

NAN: Let's play school.
DAN: Okay, let's play I'm absent.

What is yellow, has wheels and lies on its back?
A dead school bus.

How do bees get to school?
By school buzz.

What would happen if you took the school bus home?
The police would make you bring it back.

What is the difference between a school bus driver and a cold?

One knows the stops and the other stops the nose.

A class has a top and a bottom. What lies between?

The student body.

MOTHER: How do you like your new teacher?
JUNIOR: I don't. She told me to sit up front for the present and then she didn't give me one.

SUE: Does your teacher like you?
LEW: *Like* me! She *loves* me! Look at all the kisses she puts on my papers!

"My little sister is so smart! She's only in nursery school and she can spell her name backwards and forwards."

"Really? What's her name?"

"Anna."

SON: I'm glad you named me Timothy, Dad.
FATHER: Why?
SON: Because that's what the kids in school call me.

HENRY: What was my name in first grade?
TEACHER: Henry.
HENRY: What was my name in second grade?
TEACHER: Henry.
HENRY: Knock-knock.
TEACHER: Who's there?
HENRY: Henry.
TEACHER: Henry who?
HENRY: Don't tell me you've forgotten me already!

Knock-knock.
  Who's there?
Quiet Tina.
  Quiet Tina who?
Quiet Tina classroom, monkey wants to speak!

FLO: How did you find school today?
JOE: Oh, I just got off the bus—and there it was!

TEACHER: Freddie, are you the youngest member of your family?
FREDDIE: No, my puppy is.

ONE OF THE KIDS IN MY CLASS IS A REALLY BIG PEST.

***HOW BIG
A PEST
IS HE?***

He's such a pest, he gives aspirins a head-ache.

He's such a pest, he has more crust than Betty Crocker.

He's such a pest, people throw parties just not to have him.

He's such a pest, when he goes to the zoo, the monkeys throw peanuts at him.

He's such a pest, if he throws a boomerang, it doesn't come back.

He's such a pest, even echoes don't answer him.

TEACHER: If you don't stop making so much noise, I'll go crazy.

DUFFY: Too late, teacher. We stopped an hour ago.

TEACHER: Didn't you promise to behave?

STUDENT: Yes, sir.

TEACHER: And didn't I promise to punish you if you didn't?

STUDENT: Yes, sir, but since I broke my promise, you don't have to keep yours.

TEACHER: Who was older, David or Goliath?

STUDENT: David must have been, because he rocked Goliath to sleep.

TEACHER: What is the definition of ignorance?
ED: I don't know.
TEACHER: Correct!

TEACHER: Define the word "disease."
CARMEN: "Disease" is de grade you get below de B's.

TEACHER SAYS

Say each sentence three times quickly:

- A shapeless sash.

- Shoes and socks shock Susie.

- Which wrist watches are Swiss wrist watches?

WHEW!

TEACHER: Tommy, why do you always get so dirty?
TOMMY: Well, I'm a lot closer to the ground than you are.

HOMEWORK

HAROLD: Teacher, would you punish me for something I didn't do?

TEACHER: Of course not.

HAROLD: Good, because I didn't do my homework.

TEACHER: Did you do your homework?

ARTHUR: No, teacher.

TEACHER: Do you have an excuse?

ARTHUR: Yes. It's all my mother's fault.

TEACHER: She kept you from doing it?

ARTHUR: No, she didn't nag me enough.

TEACHER: This homework looks like your father's writing.

DWIGHT: Sure, I used his pen.

SON: Dad, I'm tired of doing homework.

FATHER: Now, son, hard work never killed anyone yet.

SON: I know, Dad, but I don't want to be the first.

TEACHER: How do you like doing homework?

PUPIL: I like doing nothing better.

IT'S LATER
THAN YOU THINK

TEACHER: Why are you late?

WEBSTER: Because of the sign.

TEACHER: What sign?

WEBSTER: The one that says, "School Ahead, Go Slow." That's what I did.

TEACHER: Why are you crawling into my classroom?

SONYA: Because you always say, "Don't anyone dare walk in late!"

TEACHER: Are you late to school again?

WENDELL: Yes, Miss Jones, but didn't you tell us it's never too late to learn?

Harry came home from school, very unhappy.

"I'm not going back tomorrow," he said.

"Why not, dear?" asked his mother.

"Well, I can't read and I can't write, and they won't let me talk, so what's the use?"

3. JEST TESTING

THE TEST PRAYER

Now I lay me down to rest,
I pray to pass tomorrow's test.
If I should die before I wake,
That's one less test I'll have to take.

TEACHER: I hope I didn't see you looking at Don's paper.
RON: I hope you didn't either.

TEACHER: Seymour, you copied from Elmo's paper, didn't you?
SEYMOUR: How did you find out?
TEACHER: Elmo's paper says, "I don't know," and yours says, "Me neither."

D: Great news! The teacher said we'd have a test today rain or shine!

RED: What's so great about that?

TED: It's snowing!

What would you get if you crossed a vampire and a teacher?

Lots of blood tests.

What kinds of tests do they give witches?

Hex-aminations.

FATHER: What did the teacher think of your idea?

JUNIOR: She took it like a lamb.

FATHER: Really? What did she say?

JUNIOR: Baa!

FATHER: How were the exam questions?
SON: Easy.
FATHER: Then why do you look so unhappy?
SON: The questions didn't give me any trouble—just the answers.

FATHER: How did the exams go?
SON: I got nearly 100 in every subject.
FATHER: What do you mean—nearly 100?
SON: Well—I got the naughts.

GARY: I don't think I deserve a zero on this test.
TEACHER: I agree, but it's the lowest mark I can give you.

MOTHER: Why did you get such a low mark on that test?
JUNIOR: Because of absence.
MOTHER: You mean you were absent on the day of the test?
JUNIOR: No, but the kid who sits next to me was.

FATHER: It says here that you're at the bottom in a class of 20. That's terrible.
JUNIOR: It could be worse.
FATHER: I don't see how.
JUNIOR: It could have been a bigger class.

FATHER: Aren't you first in anything at school?
JUNIOR: Sure, Dad. I'm first out when the bell rings!

FATHER: Why are your marks so low?

SON: Because I sit in the last row of the class.

FATHER: What difference does that make?

SON: Well, when the teacher hands out marks, there just aren't enough good ones left for the people in the back.

MOTHER: Why have your grades been so low since the holidays?

BARBARA: Well, Mother, you know how everything gets marked down after Christmas.

TEACHER: Do you know why you have such poor grades?

STUDENT: I can't think.

TEACHER: Exactly!

TEACHER: Have you had your eyes checked lately?

DIGBY: No, they've always been plain brown.

REPORT CARDS

STANLEY (*after the teacher handed out the report cards*): I don't want to scare you, teacher, but my father said that if I didn't bring home a good report card, *somebody* was going to get spanked!

FATHER: Look at these bills! Taxes, rent, telephone, clothes, food! The cost of everything keeps going up. I'd like to see just one thing going down.
SON: Dad, here's my report card.

FATHER: Junior, what does this "C" on your report card mean?
JUNIOR: Colossal!

SYLVIA: Dad, can you write in the dark?
FATHER: I think so. What do you want me to write?
SYLVIA: Your name on this report card.

FATHER: What a terrible report card! What's the matter with you?
MORRIS: I'm not sure, sir, if it's heredity or environment.

TEACHER SAYS

Say each sentence three times quickly:

- Dick kicks sticky bricks.

- Shave a single shingle thin.

- Stick six thick sticks there.

Did you hear about the little kid who copied from his friend's arithmetic test paper by using a mirror? He got all his answers backwards. His friend got a grade of 93 and he got 39.

TEACHER: Young man, are you the teacher of this class?

STUDENT: No, ma'am.

TEACHER: Then don't talk like an idiot!

SECOND-GRADER: I really liked being in your class, Miss Jones. I'm sorry you're not smart enough to teach us next year.

4. SHOW & TELL

TEACHER SAYS

Name the picture:

BOO!

OUCH! OUCH! OUCH!

C - A - T

LU NCH

Answers on the next page

Acute Angle

School Spirit

Vicious Circle

Windowpanes

Spelling Bee

Lunch Break

High School

Well-Rounded Education

TEACHER: Where do bugs go in winter?

HERBERT: Search me.

TEACHER: No, thanks, I just wondered if you knew.

LIBRARIAN: Sssshhh! The people next to you can't read.

SECOND-GRADER: What a shame! I've been reading since last year.

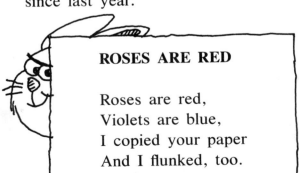

ROSES ARE RED

Roses are red,
Violets are blue,
I copied your paper
And I flunked, too.

TEACHER: Laura, why are you laughing?

LAURA: I'm sorry—I was just thinking of something.

TEACHER: Once and for all, Laura, remember that during school hours you're not supposed to think!

TEACHER: Sheldon, what are you doing? Are you learning anything?

SHELDON: No, teacher, I'm listening to you.

"I've changed my mind."
"Good, let's hope this one works better."

ELWOOD: May I bring my pet hen to school?

TEACHER: No, I've heard enough fowl language.

TEACHER: Where do blue eggs come from?
PATSY: From sad chickens.

TEACHER: Why do chickens lay eggs?
RAMONA: Because if they dropped them, they would break.

VERN: Why was the baby chicken thrown out of school?
FERN: It was caught peeping during a test.

NAN: How do you treat an injured bird?
DAN: Give it first-aid tweet-ment.

LENORE: How do they grade chickens?
TEACHER: They give them eggs-ams (exams).

TEACHER: Emma, spell mouse.
EMMA: M-O-U-S.
TEACHER: Yes—and what's on the end of it?
EMMA: A tail?

What would happen if an elephant sat in front of you in class?
You'd never see the blackboard.

SAL: Where are you taking that skunk?
VAL: To school.
SAL: What about the smell?
VAL: Oh, he'll get used to it.

What do you get if you cross a bear and a skunk?
Winnie-the-Phew (Pooh)!

TEACHER: Wendy, why do you look over your eye-glasses instead of through them?
WENDY: So I won't wear them out.

During Show and Tell, Miss Johnson showed pictures of different birds.

"George," she said, "what kind of bird do you like best?"

George thought for a while. "Fried chicken," he replied.

ANDREW: I'm teacher's pet.
MOTHER: How come?
ANDREW: She can't afford a dog.

MARK: Is your teacher strict?
TIM: I don't know. I'm too scared to ask.

(At party) "Will you pass the nuts, teacher?"

"No, I think I'll flunk them."

"I will now illustrate what I have in mind," said the teacher as she erased the blackboard.

TEACHER: Emily, this apple you gave me has some strange marks on it.
EMILY: Well, so does the report card you gave me.

SON: Dad, I know how you can save money.

FATHER: That's fine, Son. How?

SON: You remember you promised me $5 if I got passing grades?

FATHER: Yes.

SON: Well, you don't have to pay me.

SON: Good news, Dad!

FATHER: What do you mean?

SON: You won't have to buy me any new books next year. I'm taking all of this year's work over again.

TEACHER: Well, at least there's one thing I can say about your son.

FATHER: What's that?

TEACHER: With grades like these, he couldn't be cheating.

DON'T WORRY

Don't worry if your grades are low
And your rewards are few.
Remember that the mighty oak
Was once a nut like you.

TEACHER: Where do they weigh whales?
RAY: At a whale weigh station.

TEACHER: Where do they weigh fish?
STEPHANIE: On their scales.

TEACHER: Where do fish sleep?
KEVIN: In water beds.

TEACHER: Where do fish wash?
SEAN: In river basins.

TEACHER: In this box, I have a 10-foot snake.
SAMMY: You can't fool me, teacher. Snakes don't
    have feet.

ONE OF THE KIDS IN MY SCHOOL IS REALLY MEAN.

HOW MEAN IS HE?

He's so mean, he makes the teacher stay after school.

He's so mean, his parents ran away from home.

He's so mean, when he comes to school, the teacher plays hookey.

He's so mean, when he tried to join the human race, he was turned down.

He's so mean, when he graduated from high school, they gave him a no-class ring.

He's so mean, they named a cake after him—crumb!

HYGIENE TEACHER: How can you prevent diseases caused by biting insects?

JOSÉ: Don't bite any.

TEACHER: An anonymous person is one who doesn't wish to be known.

STUDENT: What a stupid definition!

TEACHER: Who said that?

STUDENT: An anonymous person.

TEACHER: Johnny, why did you kick Bobby in the stomach?

JOHNNY: It was his own fault, teacher. He turned around.

"Some kids are bad, but you're an exception."

"Really?"

"Yes, exceptionally bad."

BOB: I love to tinker around in the workshop.

ROB: That doesn't surprise me. You're the biggest tinker I know.

5. READING & WRITING & RIDDLING

TEACHER: What are you writing, Tommy?

TOMMY: A letter to myself.

TEACHER: What does it say?

TOMMY: I don't know. I won't get it till tomorrow.

TEACHER: Where is your pencil, Harmon?

HARMON: I ain't got none.

TEACHER: How many times have I told you not to say that, Harmon? Now listen: I do not have a pencil. You do not have a pencil. They do not have a pencil. Now, do you understand?

HARMON: Not really. What happened to all the pencils?

NIT: Want to hear the story about the broken pencil?

WIT: No, thanks, I'm sure it has no point.

TEACHER: Why do they say the pen is mightier than the sword?

CLASS COMEDIAN: Because no one has yet invented a ballpoint sword.

TEACHER: Dorothy, what did you write your report on?

DOROTHY: A piece of paper.

Sammy did a report about the phone book. He wrote: "This book hasn't got much of a plot, but boy, what a cast!"

Mrs. Johnson asked the class to write a composition about what they would do if they had a million dollars.

Everyone except Fannie began to write. Fannie twiddled her thumbs and looked out the window.

When Mrs. Johnson collected the papers, Fannie's sheet was blank.

"Fannie," said Mrs. Johnson, "everyone has written two pages or more, but you've done *nothing*. Why is that?"

"Nothing is what I'd do," replied Fannie, "if I had a million dollars."

TEACHER (*holding book report*): Elwood, your ideas are like diamonds.

ELWOOD: You mean they're so valuable?

TEACHER: No, I mean they're so rare.

TEACHER: Patricia, the story you handed in called "Our Dog," is exactly like your brother's.

PATRICIA: Of course. It's the same dog.

TEACHER: Howard, your poem is the worst in the class. It's not only ungrammatical, it's rude and in bad taste. I'm going to send your father a note about it.

HOWARD: I don't think that would help, teacher. He wrote it.

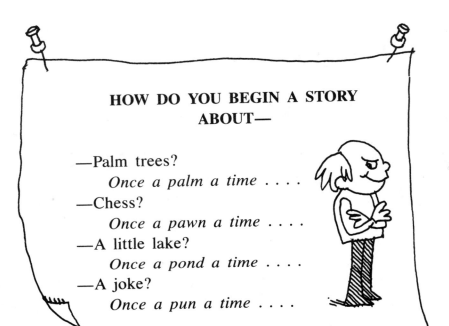

HOW DO YOU BEGIN A STORY ABOUT—

—Palm trees?
Once a palm a time . . . .
—Chess?
Once a pawn a time . . . .
—A little lake?
Once a pond a time . . . .
—A joke?
Once a pun a time . . . .

TEACHER: What does "coincidence" mean?
TRACY: Funny, I was just going to ask you that.

TEACHER: Define "procrastination."
PAM: May I answer that question tomorrow?

TEACHER: How nice that you have your new glasses, William. Now you'll be able to read everything.
WILLIAM: You mean, I don't have to come to school anymore?

TEACHER: Rhonda, please explain the difference between sufficient and enough.
RHONDA: If my mother helps me to cake, I get sufficient. If I help myself, I get enough.

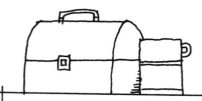

TEACHER: Your spelling is much better, Ronald. Only five mistakes that time.

RONALD: Thank you, Miss Smith.

TEACHER: Now let's go on to the next word.

TEACHER: George, how many "i"s do you use to spell Mississippi?

GEORGE: None. I can do it blindfolded.

TEACHER: Mort, how do you spell Mississippi?

MORT: The river or the state?

TEACHER: Whitney, spell "rain."

WHITNEY: R-A-N-E.

TEACHER: That's the worst spell of rain we've had around here in a long time!

TEACHER: Carlos, how do you spell "imbecile?"

CARLOS: I-M-B-U-S-L.

TEACHER: The dictionary spells it "I-M-B-E-C-I-L-E."

CARLOS: Yes, teacher, but you asked me how *I* spelled it.

SILLY SENTENCES

The teacher asked for sentences using the word "beans."

"My father grows beans," said a girl.

"My mother cooks beans," said a boy.

Then a third child spoke up, "We're all human beans (beings)," he said.

TEACHER: Charles, use the word "knock-wurst" in a sentence.

CHARLES: A chicken joke is bad; an elephant joke is worse, but I'd rate a knock-knockwurst (a knock-knock worst).

TEACHER: Ellen, give me a sentence starting with "I."

ELLEN: I is . . . .

TEACHER: No, Ellen. Always say "I am."

ELLEN: All right. "I am the ninth letter of the alphabet."

TEACHER: Max, use "defeat," "defense" and "detail" in a sentence.

MAX: The rabbit cut across the field, and defeat went over defense before detail.

AWFUL ALPHABETS

TEACHER: Alvin, how many letters are there in the alphabet?

ALVIN: 18.

TEACHER: Wrong, there are 26.

ALVIN: No, teacher, there used to be 26, but ET went home in a UFO and the CIA went after them.

TEACHER: Max, how many letters are there in the alphabet?

SANCHO: Eleven.

TEACHER: Eleven!

SANCHO: T-H-E A-L-P-H-A-B-E-T—11!

How do they say good-bye using the alphabet?

A B C'ing you!

How do they say good-bye in England?

B B C'ing you!

How do they say good-bye on the Johnny Carson Show?

N B C'ing you!

GARBLED GRAMMAR

TEACHER: If "can't" is short for "cannot," what is "don't" short for?

NATALIE: Doughnut.

JOHNNY: Him and me helped clean up the yard.

TEACHER: Now, Johnny, don't you mean he and I helped?

JOHNNY: No, Mr. Smith, you weren't even there.

TEACHER: Sylvia, what are subordinate clauses?

SYLVIA: Santa's helpers.

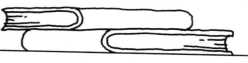

TEACHER: Rudolph, describe a synonym.
RUDOLPH: A word you use when you can't spell the other word.

TEACHER: Herman, name two pronouns.
HERMAN: Who, me?
TEACHER: Correct!

TEACHER: Wade, give me an example of a double negative.
WADE: I don't know none.
TEACHER: Excellent!

BURT: I ain't going.
TEACHER: That is not correct. Listen: I am not going. We are not going. You are not going. They are not going. Now do you understand?
BURT: Sure, teacher. Nobody ain't going.

MRS. JONES (*to the class*): Can anyone tell me the imperative of the verb "to go?" (*No reply.*)
MRS. JONES: Go, class, go!
CLASS: Thanks, Mrs. Jones! See you tomorrow!

CANDIDATES FOR THE LONGEST WORD IN THE ENGLISH LANGUAGE

Smiles
Because there's a mile between the first and last letter.

Rubber
Because it stretches.

Post Office
Because it has the most letters.

Equator
Because it circles the globe.

How is an English teacher like a judge?
They both hand out sentences.

TEACHER: Toby, what are you doing under your desk?
TOBY: Didn't you tell us to read Dr. Jekyll and Hyde (hide)?

What is an autobiography?
A car's life story.

Baker's Men by Pat E. Cake

The Making of a Hot Dog by Frank Furter

How to Raise Lambs by Shep Hurd

A History of Valentines by Bea Mine

How to Make an Igloo by S. K. Moe

Bell-Ringing by Paula D. Rope

The Nasty Kid by Enid A. Spanking

Basic Math by Adam Upp

Grade School Is Easy by Ella Mann Tree

How to Keep Things Oiled by Russ T. Gates

All About Weeds by Dan D. Lyons

Playing in the School Band by Clara Nette

LIBRARY SKILLS

"Please hush," said the librarian to some noisy children. "The people around you can't read."

"Really?" asked one little girl. "Then why are they here?"

Melvin took a book from the library because the cover read "How to Hug."

It turned out to be Volume VII of an encyclopedia.

Why do snobs like books?
Because they have titles.

What famous book is about young cats?
"A Tale of Two Kitties" (Cities).

Where is the best place to find books about trees?
In a branch library.

What reference book lists famous owls?
"Whoo's Who."

What would you get if you crossed a book of nursery rhymes and an orange?
Mother Juice (Goose).

Have you read Shakespeare?
No.
Have you read Poe?
No.
Have you read Longfellow?
No.
I give up. What have you read?
I have red suspenders.

What part of a book is like a fish?
The fin-ish.

How does a book about zombies begin?
With a dead-ication.

How do you begin a book about ducks?
With an intro-duck-tion.

SAID A BOY

Said a boy to his teacher one day,
"Wright has not written 'rite' right, I say."
    So the teacher replied,
    As the error she eyed,
"Right. Wright, write 'rite' right right
away."

NIT: Did you hear about the riot in the library?

WIT: No, what happened?

NIT: Someone found "dynamite" in the dictionary.

LIBRARIAN: Will you two please stop passing notes!

STUDENT: We're not passing notes. We're playing cards.

6. IS THIS ASSEMBLY NECESSARY?

The principal was annoyed by the noise during the assembly program.

"There seem to be several idiots in the auditorium this morning," he snapped. "Wouldn't it be better to hear one at a time?"

A voice shouted, "Okay—you start."

The person who said all things must end never heard my principal talk.

My principal is so boring, when he gives a speech even your feet fall asleep.

Until I heard my principal talk I thought my butter knife was dull.

Until I heard my principal talk, I thought water was colorless.

DIT: Where is the principal?

DOT: He's round in front.

DIT: I know what he looks like. I was just wondering where he went.

What do you get if you cross one principal with another principal?

Don't do it. Principals don't like to be crossed.

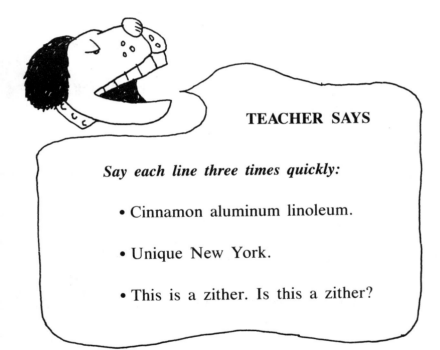

TEACHER SAYS

Say each line three times quickly:

• Cinnamon aluminum linoleum.

• Unique New York.

• This is a zither. Is this a zither?

"Wise men hesitate," said the principal. "Only fools are certain."

"Is that true?"

"I'm certain."

HAPPY HOLIDAY

How many months have 28 days?
All of them.

NIT: What comes before March?
WIT: Forward!

How many seconds are there in a year?
Twelve. January 2nd, February 2nd, March 2nd . . . .

NICK: What is there in December that isn't in any other month?
VIC: The letter "D"!

TEACHER: Why do bells ring at Christmas?
PETER: Because someone pulls the rope.

TEACHER: What does the Christmas tree stand for?
SKEETER: It would take too much room lying down.

TEACHER: What nationality is Santa Claus?
DENNIS: North Polish.

TEACHER: Why is there a Mother's Day and a Father's Day, but no Son's Day?

PUPIL: Because there is a Sunday (Son-day) every week.

Before Thanksgiving a first-grade teacher asked her pupils to tell what they were thankful for.

"I'm thankful," said one small boy, "that I'm not a turkey."

THAT'S WHAT YOU THINK!

TOM

"What did you think of the ventriloquist?" the teacher asked one of her first-graders after the show in the school auditorium.

"He wasn't very good," replied the first-grader. "But the little guy on his knee was terrific."

TEACHER: Doris, what are you going to do in the school talent show?

DORIS: Imitations.

TEACHER: Let's hear them.

DORIS: "I love you—ouch! I love you—ouch!"

TEACHER: I give up—what are you imitating?

DORIS: Two porcupines kissing.

TEACHER: Boris, what are you going to do in the school talent show?

BORIS: Bird imitations.

TEACHER: Are you going to warble?

BORIS: No, I'm going to eat worms.

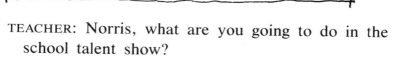

What musical key do cows sing in?
Beef-flat (B♭).

TEACHER: Norris, what are you going to do in the school talent show?

NORRIS: I'm going to sing "Old Lady River."

TEACHER: Don't you mean "Old Man River"?

NORRIS: No, I'm singing about a lady river—Mississippi!

DELORES (*after singing a song horribly*): How did you like my execution?

MUSIC TEACHER: I'm all in favor of it.

MUSIC TEACHER (TO VOICE STUDENT)

I didn't say your voice was out of this world—I said it was unearthly.

You have a fine voice. Don't spoil it by singing.

I like the song you sang. One day you should put it to music.

You sing like a bird—a screech owl!

I've heard better sounds coming from a leaking balloon.

Every time I tear a rag, it reminds me of your voice.

You couldn't carry a tune if it had a handle.

Of course your voice is pure. You strain it every time you sing.

You're a natural musician. Your tongue is sharp and your head is flat.

VOICE TEACHER: Now, please sing the scale.

STUDENT: Do-re-mi-fa-sol-la-do.

VOICE TEACHER: You left out the "ti."

STUDENT: I know—every time I try to hit a high note, my voice sinks.

VOICE TEACHER: Again you left out the "t."

TEACHER: What are your favorite songs?

GORDON: I have five of them—"Three Blind Mice" and "Tea for Two."

(*Overheard in the school auditorium at a glee club performance*):

"Is that a popular song?"

"It was before today."

"That tune has been running through my head all day."

"Of course—there's nothing there to get in its way."

PUPIL (*at concert*): What is the book the orchestra leader is looking at?

TEACHER: That's the score.

PUPIL: Really? Who's winning?

Why did George bring a ladder to the assembly program?

The music teacher asked him to sing higher.

STUDENT (*after playing the piano*): I've never had a lesson in my life—and I can prove it.
MUSIC TEACHER: Never mind, you just did.

MUSIC TEACHER: Why did you put that vegetable on the piano?
STUDENT: You told me my playing would improve if I had a beet (beat)!

BAND STUDENT: Our high school band played Beethoven yesterday.
ATHLETE: Who won?

The class laughed when I sat down at the piano—no stool.

The class laughed when I sat down at the piano with my hands tied behind my back. They didn't know I played by ear.

How do you clean a tuba?
With a tuba toothpaste!

"Look at how gracefully that girl eats her corn on the cob," said Mrs. Jones to her son, Harry, at the restaurant.

"Of course," Harry replied, "she plays the flute in the school band."

7. WAY OUT TO LUNCH

What is the worst thing you're likely to find in the school cafeteria?
The food.

The food in our school cafeteria is perfect, if you happen to be a termite.

The food in our school cafeteria is so bad, you get a prescription with every meal.

The food in our school cafeteria is so bad, flies go there to commit suicide.

"What is this on my plate in case I have to describe it to my doctor?"

"Is that school food spicy?"
   "No, smoke always comes out of my ears."

What did the computer do in the lunchroom?
It had a byte.

LITTLE MONSTER: Mother, I hate my teacher.
MOTHER MONSTER: Then just eat your salad, dear.

MOTHER: Why on earth did you swallow the money I gave you?
JUNIOR: You said it was my lunch money.

TEACHER: What is a mushroom?
MAXWELL: The place they store the school food.

TEACHER SAYS

Say each sentence three times quickly:

- A cupcake cook's cap.

- For cheap sheep soup, shoot sheep.

- Cheeky chimps chomp cheap chop suey.

TEACHER: When do astronauts eat?
SCOTT: At launch time.

What do astronauts eat from?
Flying saucers.

What gets served at science fairs?
Fish 'n' chips (fission chips).

What kind of food do math teachers eat?
Square meals.

Where do math teachers go to eat?
To the lunch counter.

Where do smart frankfurters end up?
On the honor roll.

LITTLE BOY (*opening lunch bag*): Not again! Day after day, the same old thing—cheese sandwiches on white bread. I'm sick and tired of them.

TEACHER: Why don't you ask your mother to make a different kind of sandwich for you?

LITTLE BOY: I can't.

TEACHER: Why not?

LITTLE BOY: Because my mother doesn't make them—I do.

TEACHER: What does an 800-pound gorilla eat?

PUPIL: Anything it wants.

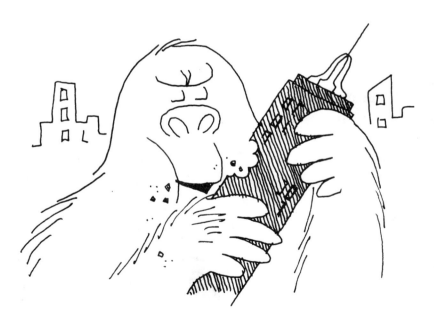

BARRY: Ugh—this plate is wet.

CARY: That's the soup.

My school cafeteria is a place where they serve soup to nuts.

"I thought this was barley soup—not barely soup!"

NIT: I thought this was supposed to be pea soup, but it tastes like soap!
WIT: Oh, it must be tomato soup. Pea soup tastes like gasoline.

"Why do you have alphabet soup every day for lunch?"
"So I can eat and practise reading at the same time."

What happened to the bad egg in the lunchroom?
It got eggs-pelled.

NIT: Do you feel like a doughnut?
WIT: Of course not, do I look like one?

What is the difference between a teacher and a doughnut?
You can't dunk a teacher in a glass of milk.

TEACHER: There is a general belief that fish is brain food.
KIRK: Yes, teacher, I eat it all the time.
TEACHER: Oh, well, there goes another scientific theory.

TEACHER SAYS

*Say each sentence
three times quickly:*

- Fred's fish-and-chip shop.

- Find Mrs. Fine's fine fish-sauce shop.

- Three free fruit floats.

- A big baker bakes black bread.

- Blend the blue-black blueberries.

- A box of biscuits, a box of mixed biscuits and a biscuit mixer.

TEACHER: Order, children! Order!
CLASS COMEDIAN: I'll have a burger with French fries.

I feel like a sandwich.
    Funny, you look like a pork chop.

I feel like a piece of chocolate.
    Well, stick around. If I get hungry, I'll bite you.

IKE: There's a fly in this ice cream.
SPIKE: Serves him right. Let him freeze!

LEM: Is this peach or apple pie?
CLEM: If you can't tell by the taste, what difference does it make?

ART: That crust on the apple pie was tough.
BART: That wasn't the crust. That was the paper plate.

"If I cut an apple in two, what would I get?"
  "Two pieces."
"If I cut a pear in four, what would I get?"
  "Four pieces."
"If I cut a banana in eight, what would I get?"
  "Eight pieces."
"Now, if all the pieces were added together, what would I get?"
  "Fruit salad!"

TEACHER: How do you make Mexican chili?
PUPIL: Take him to the North Pole.

TEACHER: How do you make meat loaf?
PUPIL: Send it on a vacation.

TEACHER: Why is that pickle behind your ear?
PUPIL: Gosh! I must have eaten my pencil!

FLOYD: Is a chicken big enough to eat when it's two weeks old?

TEACHER: Of course not!

FLOYD: Then how does it manage to live?

ONE OF THE GIRLS IN MY SCHOOL IS TERRIBLY CONCEITED.

HOW CONCEITED IS SHE?

She's so conceited, she goes out in the garden so the flowers can smell her.

She holds her nose so high in the air, there's an inch of snow on it.

She holds her nose so high in the air that every time she sneezes, she wets the ceiling.

She holds her nose so high in the air that every time she hiccups, she blows her hat off.

8. IT'S A FUNNY WORLD

"It's clear," said the teacher, "that you haven't studied your geography. What's your excuse?"

"Well—my dad says the world is changing every day. So I decided to wait a little while until it settles down."

TEACHER: Josh, what can you tell us about the Dead Sea?

JOSH: I didn't even know it was sick!

TEACHER: What are the small rivers that run into the Nile?

GRACE: The Juve-niles!

TEACHER: Why is the Mississippi such an unusual river?

SYLVESTER: Because it has four eyes and can't see.

TEACHER: What are the Great Plains?

PIP: The 747s.

TEACHER: Where is the English Channel?
ALEX: I don't know. My television set doesn't pick it up.

GERTRUDE: My teacher was mad because I didn't know where the Andes were.
MOTHER: Well, dear, next time remember where you put things.

Why does the Statue of Liberty stand in New York Harbor?
Because it can't sit down.

TEACHER: Is Lapland heavily populated?
BRUCE: No, there are not many Lapps to the mile.

TEACHER: Name an animal that lives in Lapland.
PUPIL: A reindeer.
TEACHER: Good. Now name another.
PUPIL: Another reindeer.

TEACHER: Rachel, can you tell us where elephants are found?
RACHEL: We don't have to find elephants. They're so big, they don't get lost.

TEACHER: Rupert, what fur do we get from the leopard?
RUPERT: As fur as possible.

ERNIE: I only got 35 in Arithmetic and 50 in Spelling, but I knocked them cold in Geography.
BERNIE: What did you get?
ERNIE: Zero.

TEACHER: What birds are found in Portugal?
ALVIN: Portu-geese.

TEACHER: Name three famous Poles.
CLASS COMEDIAN: North, South and tad.

What do we do with crude oil?
Teach it manners.

TEACHER SAYS

Say each sentence three times quickly:

- She sheared six shabby sheep.

- Do sheep shun sunshine?

- The sixth sick sheik's sixth sheep's sick.

- Cheap ship trips.

- Sure the ship's shipshape, sir.

- The seething sea ceaseth seething.

Herman's teacher always rewarded good work by putting a gold star at the top of her students' homework. One day Herman came home with a big zero at the top of his paper.

"Herman, what does this mean?" asked his mother.

"Oh," Herman explained, "my teacher ran out of stars, so she gave me a moon."

What do frogs like to sit on?
Toadstools.

What do frogs wear on their feet?
Open-toed (toad) shoes.

How do you get nuts from a squirrel?
Walk up to the squirrel and say, "This is a stickup!"

TEACHER: Do sailors go on safaris?
PUPIL: Not safaris (so far as) I know.

TEACHER: What is an island?
RUTHIE: An island is a piece of land surrounded by water except in one place.
TEACHER: What place is that?
RUTHIE: On top.

Knock-knock.
   Who's there?
Oscar and Greta.
   Oscar and Greta who?
Oscar foolish question,
Greta foolish answer.

Knock-knock.
   Who's there?
Summertime.
   Summertime who?
Summertime I get the right answer
and summertime I don't.

TEACHER (*correcting a pupil*): When I asked you what shape the world was in, I meant "round" or "flat"—not "rotten."

TEACHER: Danny, give me three reasons why you know the earth is round.
DANNY: Because my mother says so, my father says so—and you say so.

"Dorrie, do you know a girl named Louise?"
"Yes, Mom, she sleeps next to me in Geography."

9. MATH-A-RAMA

FLIP: I failed every subject except algebra.
FLOP: How did you keep from failing that?
FLIP: I didn't take algebra.

TEACHER: Are you good at math?
PUPIL: Yes and no.
TEACHER: What does that mean?
PUPIL: Yes, I'm no good in math.

"Pop, will you help me find the lowest common denominator in this problem?"

"Good heavens, don't tell me they haven't found it yet! They were looking for it when I was a boy!"

TEACHER: Lisa, did your father help you with these math problems?
LISA: No, teacher. I got them wrong all by myself.

"Teacher, I can't do this problem."

"Any five-year-old should be able to do that problem."

"No wonder I can't do it! I'm almost ten!"

COUNTING TO 10

The teacher was reviewing counting with her first-grade class.

"Pauline," she asked, "can you count to 10 without mistakes?"

"Yes," said Pauline, and she did.

"Now, Philo," said the teacher, "can you count from 10 to 20?"

"That depends," said Philo, "with or without mistakes?"

TEACHER: Can you count to 10?

SUZANNE: Yes, teacher. (*counting on her fingers at waist level*) One, two, three, four, five, six, seven, eight, nine, ten.

TEACHER: Good. Now can you count higher?

SUZANNE: Yes, teacher. (*She puts her hands over her head and counts on her fingers.*) One, two, three, four, five, six, seven, eight, nine, ten.

TEACHER: Can you count to 10?

ERIC: Yes, teacher—one, two, three, four, five, six, seven, eight, nine, ten.

TEACHER: Now go on from there.

ERIC: Jack, Queen, King.

TEACHER: What is two and two?

HUGH: Four.

TEACHER: That's good.

HUGH: Good? It's perfect!

TEACHER: If one and one make two, and two and two make four, how much do four and four make?

ANNIE: That's not fair, Teacher. You answer the easy ones yourself and leave the hard ones for us.

TEACHER: How much is half of eight?

WENDELL: Up and down or across?

TEACHER: What do you mean?

WENDELL: Up and down it's 3 and across it's 0.

TEACHER: Now, class, whatever I ask, I want you to answer at once. Amy, how much is eight and eight?

AMY: At once!

TEACHER: If there were 10 cats in a boat, and one jumped out, how many would be left?

MARYLOU: None, because they were all copycats.

TEACHER: If you received $10 from 10 people, what would you get?

SASHA: A new bike.

Why was the math book unhappy?
It had too many problems.

TEACHER: If I lay one egg here and another there, how many eggs will there be?

CLARK: None!

TEACHER (*surprised*): Why not?

CLARK: Because you can't lay eggs!

TEACHER: Stella, take 932 from 1,439. What is the difference?

STELLA: That's what I say—what's the difference?

Who invented fractions?
Henry the Eighth.

"Our teacher has a bad memory. For three days she asked us how much is two and two. We told her it was four. But she still doesn't know. Today she asked us again."

MYSTERY

Birds on the mountain,
Fish in the sea,
How you passed math
Is a mystery to me.

HECTOR: I've added these figures ten times.
TEACHER: Good work!
HECTOR: And here are my ten answers.

Why is a dog with a lame leg like adding 6 and 7?
He puts down the three and carries the one.

Why is six afraid of seven?
Because seven eight (ate) nine.

What animal is best at math?
Rabbits—they multiply fastest.

DIT: My dog is great at math.
DOT: Really?
DIT: Ask him how much is two minus two.
DOT: But two minus two is nothing!
DIT: That's what he'll answer—nothing!

TEACHER: If I gave you three rabbits today and five rabbits tomorrow, how many rabbits would you have?

WENDY: Nine.

TEACHER: Sorry Wendy, you'd have eight.

WENDY: No, Teacher, I'd have nine. I already have one rabbit at home.

TEACHER: If you add 3452 and 3096, then divide the answer by 4 and multiply by 6, what would you get?

LILY: The wrong answer.

FATHER: How are you doing in arithmetic?

DIRK: I've learned to add up the zeros, but the numbers are still giving me trouble.

What makes arithmetic hard work?
All those numerals you have to carry.

JASON: I got 100 in school today.

MOTHER: Wonderful. What did you get 100 in?

JASON: Two things: I got 50 in Spelling and 50 in History.

MOTHER (*sighing*): Well, at least you can add.

PAMELA: I got 100 in an arithmetic test and still didn't pass.

FATHER: Why not, for goodness sake?

PAMELA: Because the answer was 200.

Why are misers good math teachers?
They know how to make every penny count.

What kind of tree does a math teacher climb?
Geometry.

What do you have to know to get top grades in geometry?
All the angles.

What kind of pliers do you use in arithmetic?
Multipliers.

TEACHER: Vincent, if you had one dollar and you asked your father for another, how many dollars would you have?
VINCENT: One dollar.
TEACHER (*sadly*): You don't know your arithmetic.
VINCENT (*sadly*): You don't know my father.

Lucille stood quietly as her father examined her report card.

"What is this 45 in math?" asked her father.

"I think that's the size of the class," she said quickly.

FATHER: If I had five coconuts and I gave you three, how many would I have left?

FRANKIE: I don't know.

FATHER: Why not?

FRANKIE: In our school we do all our arithmetic in apples and oranges.

TEACHER: If I had seven oranges in one hand and eight oranges in the other, what would I have?

CLASS COMEDIAN: Big hands!

The teacher was giving her first-grade class a quiz on counting. Naomi got things started by counting from 1 to 10.

"Now, Charles," said the teacher, "you take over, beginning with 11."

"11, 14, 23, 42, 26," said Charles.

"What kind of counting is that?" asked the teacher.

"Who's counting?" replied Charles. "I'm calling signals."

10. HISTORY HEE-HAWS

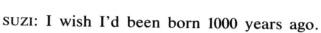

SUZI: I wish I'd been born 1000 years ago.

MOTHER: Why is that, dear?

SUZI: Just think of all the history I wouldn't have to study.

My teacher reminds me of history—she's always repeating herself.

What do history teachers make when they want to get together?
  Dates.

What do they talk about?
  The good old days.

Who was the biggest thief in history?
  Atlas, because he held up the whole world.

What was Noah's profession?
  Ark-itect.

What kind of illumination did Noah use on the ark?
  Floodlights.

The first-grade teacher brought her little pupils to the museum. They stood in front of a mummy case. At the bottom of the case were the words "1286 BC."

"Does anyone know what that number means?" asked the teacher.

One little kid spoke up, "That must be the license of the car that hit him."

FOLLOW
THAT
CAR!

Did they play tennis in ancient Egypt?
Yes, the Bible tells how Joseph served in Pharaoh's court.

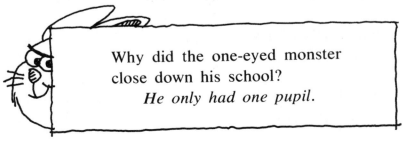

Why did the one-eyed monster close down his school?
He only had one pupil.

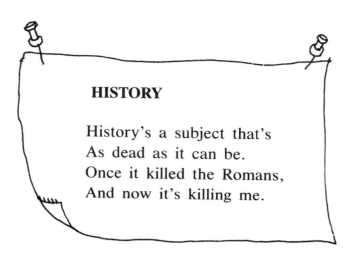

HISTORY

History's a subject that's
As dead as it can be.
Once it killed the Romans,
And now it's killing me.

TEACHER: Where did knights learn to kill dragons?
VICTOR: In knight (night) school.

TEACHER: How did Vikings communicate with each other?
HESTER: By Norse code.

What is a forum?
Two-um plus two-um.

How did Columbus's men sleep on their ships?
With their eyes shut.

What did Napoleon become when he was 41 years old?
42 years old.

How do we know Napoleon loved spicy food?
First he mustard (mustered) his army, and then he salted (assaulted) the city.

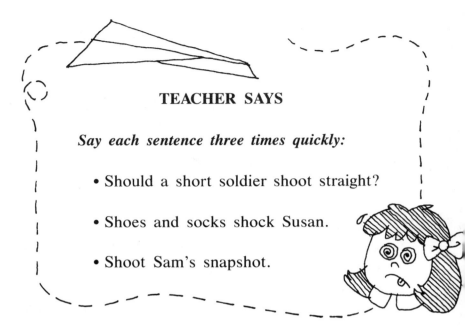

TEACHER SAYS

Say each sentence three times quickly:

• Should a short soldier shoot straight?

• Shoes and socks shock Susan.

• Shoot Sam's snapshot.

TEACHER: The Spanish explorers travelled around the world on a galleon.

CLASS COMEDIAN: How many galleons did they get to a mile?

"Class, you've been so bad, you're all going to have to stay after school," said the teacher.

"Give me liberty or give me death!" came a voice from the back of the room.

"Who said that?" snapped the teacher.

"Patrick Henry!" said the class.

TEACHER: What did Paul Revere say when he got on his horse?

HELGA: "Giddy-up!"

TEACHER: Andrea, what did they do at the Boston Tea Party?

ANDREA: I don't know, teacher, I wasn't invited.

TEACHER: Helen, what did they wear at the Boston Tea Party?

HELEN: T-shirts?

TEACHER: Where was the Declaration of Independence signed?

STANLEY: At the bottom.

TEACHER: Did the Indians hunt bear?

DONALD: Not in winter.

What is red, white and blue and says, "Ouch"?
  Betsy Ross, sewing the flag, without her eye-glasses.

What did Betsy Ross say when they asked if the flag was ready?
  "Give me a Minute, Man!"

TEACHER: Why did George Washington chop down the cherry tree?
PUPIL: I'm stumped.

TEACHER: When crossing the Delaware River, why did George Washington stand up in the boat?
CLASS COMEDIAN: He was afraid if he sat down someone would hand him an oar.

TEACHER: Why was George Washington buried at Mount Vernon?
PETER: Because he was dead.

FATHER: How did you do in your tests, Elvis?
ELVIS: I did what George Washington did.
FATHER: What's that?
ELVIS: I went down in history.

TEACHER: Carol, do you know the 20th President of the United States?
CAROL: No, we were never introduced.

"Abraham Lincoln had a hard childhood," explained the first-grade teacher. "He had to walk nearly seven miles to school every day."

"It was his own fault," said Norman. "Why couldn't he get up and catch the school bus like everybody else?"

A MYSTERY

He asked me *when?* I could not tell.
He asked me *who?* Again I fell.
He named a man, to me a stranger,
I could see myself in danger.
What was this plight—this mystery?
Oh—just my course in history.

TEACHER: Who gave the Liberty Bell to Philadelphia?

DANNY: It must have been a duck family.

TEACHER: A duck family!

DANNY: Didn't you tell us there was a quack in it?

What is the biggest telephone company in space?
ET & T (AT & T).

TEACHER: Why did the pioneers cross the country in covered wagons?

CLASS COMEDIAN: Because they didn't want to wait 40 years for a train.

FATHER: Ingrid, I see from your report card that you're not doing well in history. Why not?

INGRID: Because my teacher is always asking me about things that happened way before I was born.

FATHER: I see you've flunked history again, Junior.

JUNIOR: Yes, dad. You always told me it's best to let bygones be bygones.

WHEN I DIE

When I die, bury me deep.
Bury my history book at my feet.
Tell the teacher I've gone to rest
And won't be back for the history test.

11. STUDY HALL

PRINCIPAL: If you study hard, you'll get ahead.
SAL: No, thanks, I already have a head.

Knock-knock.
  Who's there?
Don Juan.
  Don Juan who?
Don Juan to study today.

WHY STUDY?

The more we study, the more we know,
The more we know, the more we forget,
The more we forget, the less we know,
So, why study?

PRINCIPAL: Do you believe in clubs for children?
TEACHER: If all else fails.

10 REASONS WHY I DON'T HAVE MY HOMEWORK

1. My little sister ate it.

2. I was mugged on the way to school, and the mugger took everything I had.

3. Our puppy toilet-trained on it.

4. Some creatures from outer space borrowed it so they could study how the human brain worked.

5. I put it in a safe, but lost the combination.

6. I loaned it to a friend, but he suddenly moved away.

7. Our furnace stopped working, and we had to burn it to keep from freezing.

8. I left it in my shirt, and my mother put it in the washing machine.

9. I didn't do it because I didn't want to add to your already heavy workload.

10. I lost it fighting with a kid who said you weren't the best teacher in the school.

MOTHER: Our son's teacher says he ought to have an encyclopedia.

FATHER: Why? Let him walk to school like I did.

What does an elf do when it gets home from school? *Gnomework (Homework).*

FRANK: Day after day, the boy and his dog went to school together. Then the day came when they had to part.

HANK: What happened?

FRANK: The dog graduated.

My dog is so bad,
he was expelled from
obedience school.

TEACHER SAYS

Say each sentence three times quickly:

- Big B-52 bombers.

- The back brake block broke.

- Peggy Babcock blushes.

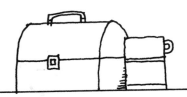

LATE AGAIN?

TEACHER: Why are you late?

LORISSA: It rained last night. The road was so wet and slippery that for every step I made forward, I slipped backwards two steps.

TEACHER: Well, if it rains again tomorrow, start walking in the opposite direction.

TEACHER: Why are you late?

AMOS: I lost my quarter.

TEACHER: And why are you late, Oliver?

OLIVER: I was standing on it.

TEACHER: Why are you late?

BARNEY: I sprained my ankle.

TEACHER: What a lame excuse!

TEACHER: Why are you late?

TIMMY: I was riding my bike and I ran into a tree.

TEACHER: Well, well, that's the first time I ever heard of sap running *into* a tree.

TEACHER: What's the idea of coming to school two hours late?

BASIL (*in bandages*): But, teacher, I was run over.

TEACHER: It doesn't take two hours to get run over.

TEACHER: Do clocks tell time?
CASSIE: No, Teacher, you have to look at them.

Why was the school clock punished?
Because it tocked (talked) too much.

TEACHER: Frieda, how long is a minute?
FRIEDA: Which kind of minute do you mean—a real minute—or "wait-a-minute"?

MOTHER (*to sleeping son*): Aldo, it's time to get up. It's twenty to eight.
ALDO: In whose favor?

THEODORE: My father beats me up every morning.
TEACHER: How terrible!
THEODORE: It's not too bad. He gets up at 7 and I get up at 8.

SOMETHING GOOD

Go on to college, continue your knowledge,
Be smart, be brave, be true.
If they make penicillin from moldy cheese,
They can make something good out of you.

ONE OF THE KIDS IN MY SCHOOL IS VERY DUMB.

HOW DUMB IS HE?

He's so dumb, the nearest he ever came to a brainstorm is a light drizzle.

He's so dumb, he cut up the calendar because he wanted to take some time off from school.

He's so dumb, he flunked recess.

He's so dumb, the only kind of poetry he can make up is blank verse.

He's so dumb, he trips over his IQ.

He's so dumb, if he were twice as smart, he'd still be a half-wit.

ONE OF THE KIDS IN MY SCHOOL IS VERY DUMB.

HOW DUMB IS HE?

He's so dumb he thinks noodle soup is brain food.

He's so dumb he pals around with morons so he can have someone to look up to.

He's so dumb he tries to blow out light bulbs.

He's so dumb, he put a rubber band around his head to stretch his mind.

He's so dumb, the only time he has something on his mind is when he wears a hat.

SCHOOL DAZE

From what school do you have to drop out in order to graduate?
Parachute school.

What school has a sign on it that says, "Please don't knock."
Karate school.

At which college can you learn how to drive tanks?
Tank U.

What do they teach vampires in business courses?
How to type blood.

TEACHER: How can you be such a perfect idiot?
EDWIN: I practise a lot.

What happened when the teacher wrote, "Please wash," on the blackboard?
The school janitor took a bath.

Why did the teacher marry the school janitor?
He swept her off her feet.

What is the difference between a teacher and a train engineer?

One trains the mind, the other minds the train.

What's the difference between a train and a teacher?

One says, "Choo-choo," and the other says, "Take the gum out of your mouth."

TEACHER: Did you take a bath today?
KERMIT: Why, is one missing?

ARNOLD: Mom, my teacher told me not to take any more baths.
MOTHER: Are you sure that's what she said?
ARNOLD: Well, she told me to stay out of hot water—or else.

TEACHER: Edna, I drove by your house yesterday and I saw your family wash in the back yard.
EDNA: You must have had the wrong house. We all wash in the bathroom.

What is green and wet and teaches school?
The Teacher from the Black Lagoon.

"Emily," said the teacher, "I don't know what I'm going to do with you. Everything goes in one ear and out the other."

"Of course," said Emily, "isn't that why we have two ears?"

FATHER: Stuart, your teacher tells me you're at the bottom of your class.

STUART: So what, Dad? We learn the same thing at both ends.

MOTHER CANNIBAL: Junior was sent home from school today.

FATHER CANNIBAL: What happened?

MOTHER CANNIBAL: They caught him buttering up the teacher.

10 MORE REASONS WHY I DON'T HAVE MY HOMEWORK

1. A sudden gust of wind blew it out of my hands, and I never saw it again.

2. I was kidnapped by terrorists and they just let me go, so I didn't have time to do it.

3. The lights in our house went out, and I had to burn it to get enough light to see the fuse box.

4. A kid fell in the lake, and I jumped in to rescue him. My homework drowned.

5. I used it to fill a hole in my shoe.

6. My father had a nervous breakdown, and he cut it up to make paper dolls.

7. My pet gerbils had babies, and they used it to make a nest.

8. I didn't do it, because I didn't want the other kids in class to look bad.

9. I made a paper airplane out of it and it got hijacked.

10. ET took it home.

The teacher was complaining about one of her pupils.

"He is one of the most difficult students I ever had," she moaned.

"How difficult can a nine-year-old possibly be?" she was asked.

"To give you an idea," replied the teacher, "his mother comes to PTA meetings in disguise."

Who belongs to the Monster PTA?
Mummies and deadies.

LESTER: Dad, there's a small PTA meeting tomorrow that you have to come to.

FATHER: If it's a small one, do I have to be there?

LESTER: I'm afraid so, Dad. It's just between you, me and my teacher.

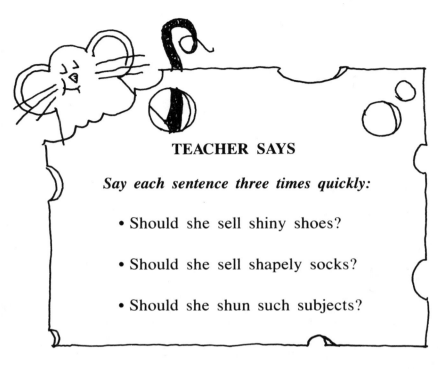

TEACHER SAYS

Say each sentence three times quickly:

- Should she sell shiny shoes?

- Should she sell shapely socks?

- Should she shun such subjects?

"No one likes me at school," said the son to his mother. "The kids don't and the teachers don't. I want to stay home."

"You have to go, son," insisted his mother. "You're not sick, and you have a lot to learn. Besides, you're 45 years old. You're the principal and you have to go to school!"

DORA: All the criticism of the American school system in newspapers and magazines is absolutely justified.

FATHER: Do you think so?

DORA: Yes, I do. And if you want proof of how bad it is, just look at the terrible marks on my report card.

NIT: Will these stairs take me to the principal's office?

WIT: No, you have to climb them.

PRINCIPAL: What is your name, young man?

BOY: Henry.

PRINCIPAL: Say "Sir."

BOY: All right. Sir Henry!

PRINCIPAL: When you grow up, Seymour, I want you to be a gentleman.

SEYMOUR: I don't want to be a gentleman, sir. I want to be just like you.

"Isn't the principal a dummy!" said a boy to a girl.

"Say, do you know who I am?" asked the girl.

"No."

"I'm the principal's daughter."

"And do you know who I am?" asked the boy.

"No," she replied.

"Thank goodness!"

Old principals never die, they just lose their faculties.

Old teachers never retire, they just lose their class.

12. RECESS RIOT

My teacher told me to exercise with dumbbells. Will you join me in the gym?

TEACHER: Why are you taking your math book to the gym?
LEONARD: I have to reduce some fractions.

TEACHER: It is well known that exercise kills germs.
CLASS COMEDIAN: But how do you get the germs to exercise?

CLASS COMEDIAN: I heard a new joke the other day. I wonder if I told it to you.
TEACHER: Was it funny?
CLASS COMEDIAN: Yes.
TEACHER: You didn't.

TEACHER: Did you make up that joke all by yourself?
CLASS COMEDIAN: Yes, out of my head.
TEACHER: You must be!

Let's talk again when your brain gets back from recess.

MORE MESSAGES FOR
THE CLASS COMEDIAN

You have a ready wit. Please let us know when it's ready.

Jokes like that will make humor illegal.

You think you're a wit? Well, you're half right.

If Adam came back to earth, the only thing he would recognize are your jokes.

That joke was so bad, you'd need a microscope to see the point.

That joke was so corny, it could feed a chicken for five years.

"What kind of marks did you get in physical education?"

"I didn't get any marks—only a few bruises."

QUENTIN: My brother is in a fight in the school yard.
PRINCIPAL (*rushing into the hall*): How long has it been going on?
QUENTIN: Half an hour, sir.
PRINCIPAL: And you're just telling me now?
QUENTIN: Well, up to now he was winning.

LITTLE FRED: Show me a tough guy and I'll show you a coward.
BIG BULLY: Well, I'm a tough guy.
LITTLE FRED: Well, I'm a coward.

PRINCIPAL: Why are you running in the hall?
SHELDON: I'm running to stop a fight.
PRINCIPAL: That's good. Between whom?
SHELDON: Between me and the guy who's chasing me!

Omar's parents were shocked by the note from his teacher. She wanted a written excuse for his presence.

The French teacher received the following note:
Please excuse my daughter from class today. Her throat is so sore, she can barely speak English.

"I think I have a cold or something in my head."
"It must be a cold."

What is the difference between a dressmaker and the school nurse?

One cuts the dresses and the other dresses the cuts.

SCHOOL NURSE: Can I take your pulse?
NIGEL: Why? Haven't you got one of your own?

Why is the school yard larger at recess?

Because there are more feet in it.

"I have the body of an athlete."
"Better give it back. You're getting it out of shape."

What athlete is never promoted?

The left back.

TEACHER SAYS

Say each sentence three times quickly:

• Surely the sun shall shine soon.

• Sascha slashes sheets slightly.

• She says she shall sew a sheet shut.

What three R's do cheerleaders learn at school?
"Rah, rah, rah!"

Why do soccer players do well in school?
Because they use their heads.

Who was the fastest runner of all time?
Adam. He was first in the human race.

What famous runner had the most peculiar trainer?
Cinderella—she had a pumpkin for a coach.

What subjects do runners like best?
Jog-raphy (geography).

ANGUS: Mom, we played baseball in school today and I stole second base.
MOTHER: Well, you march right over to school and put it back.

AARON: I went out for the football team, Dad.
FATHER: Did you make it?
AARON: I think so. The coach looked at me and said, "This is the end."

TEACHER: The national sport in Spain is bullfighting and in England it's cricket.
PERCY: I'd rather play in England.
TEACHER: Why is that?
PERCY: It's easier to fight crickets.

When do boxers start wearing gloves?
When it gets cold.

⭘⭘ ⭘ MESSAGES FROM THE COACH

Just because the world is out of shape doesn't mean you have to be, too.

You're in such bad shape, if you threw yourself on the floor you'd miss.

You're in such bad shape, you get winded playing checkers.

You're in such bad shape, you get winded when your stocking runs.

You're in such bad shape, if you tried to whip cream, the cream would win.

You're in such bad shape, you better not try to lick an envelope.

Your muscles are like potatoes—mashed potatoes.

The only regular exercise you ever get is reaching for seconds.

You'd make a great football player. Even your breath is offensive.

Geoffrey sent his father a letter from college:
    Dear Dad:
        No money. Not funny.
            Sonny.
The father wrote back:
    Dear Son:
        How sad. Too bad.
            Dad

NIT: I have a chance on the school soccer team.
WIT: I didn't know they were raffling it off.

TEACHER: Ralph, how many times have I told you not to speak without permission?
RALPH: I didn't know I had to keep score.

MOTHER: Julius, what did you learn in school today?
JULIUS: I learned to say "No, ma'am"; "Yes, sir"; and "Yes, ma'am."
MOTHER: You did?
JULIUS: Yup!

AL: My father wants me to have everything he didn't have when he was a boy.
SAL: What didn't he have?
AL: A's on his report card.

13. LAUGHTER FROM THE LAB

FRED: When I die, I'm going to leave my brain to science.

NED: That's nice. Every little bit helps.

TEACHER: Why did the germ cross the microscope?

SYLVIA: To get to the other slide.

SCIENCE QUIZ

1. What does it mean when the barometer falls?
2. How do you fix a short circuit?
3. What should you do with a dead battery?
4. How do you charge a battery?
5. Who invented spaghetti?
6. What is barium?
7. What is camphor?
8. What happens when you swallow uranium?
9. What is the difference between lightning and electricity?
10. Explain "mean temperature."

"C" BATTERY

Answers on next page.

ANSWERS TO SCIENCE QUIZ

1. That whoever nailed it up didn't do such a good job.
2. Lengthen it.
3. Bury it.
4. With a credit card.
5. A fellow who used his noodle.
6. What you do to the dead.
7. For having fun in the summer.
8. You get an atomic (stomach) ache.
9. We have to pay for electricity.
10. Ten degrees below zero when you're not wearing long johns.

R.I.P.
"A"
BATTERY

TEACHER: Who can give me a definition of claustrophobia?
SIGMUND: An unnatural fear of Santa Claus.

TEACHER: Kenneth, can you tell me what death is?
KENNETH: Patrick Henry's second choice.

TEACHER: What is stucco?
STUDENT: What you get when you sit on gum-mo?

TEACHER: How can you tell the difference between a boy moose and a girl moose?
ANITA: Er—by his mous-tache?

FAILING STUDENT: If a person's brain stops working, does he die?
TEACHER: You're alive, aren't you?

TEACHER: Name a conductor of electricity.

JOSIE: Why—er—

TEACHER: Wire is right. Name a unit of electrical power.

JOSIE: What?

TEACHER: The watt is absolutely correct.

TEACHER: How did Edison's invention of electricity affect society?

SHEP: If it weren't for him, we'd have to watch television by candlelight!

EARTH SCIENCE QUIZ
1. What is a magnetic field?
2. What kind of rocks look alike?
3. What is a geyser?
4. What is a volcano?
5. What is the center of gravity?
6. Where is the ocean deepest?
7. Why is the ocean full of salt?
8. Why does the ocean roar?

Answers on next page.

What is the difference between ammonia and pneumonia?

Ammonia comes in bottles, pneumonia comes in chests.

TEACHER: Linda, what is a vacuum?

LINDA: I can't think of it just now, but I've got it in my head.

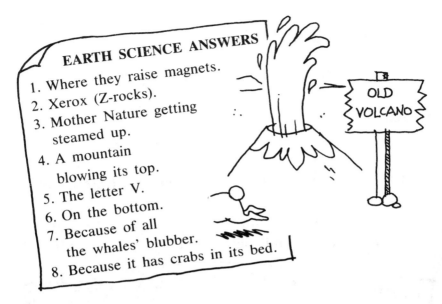

EARTH SCIENCE ANSWERS

1. Where they raise magnets.
2. Xerox (Z-rocks).
3. Mother Nature getting steamed up.
4. A mountain blowing its top.
5. The letter V.
6. On the bottom.
7. Because of all the whales' blubber.
8. Because it has crabs in its bed.

Did you hear about the deer who took a test?
He did so well, the teacher passed the buck.

TEACHER: How fast does light travel?
MARCEL (*yawning*): I don't know, teacher, but it gets here too early in the morning.

TEACHER: Eric, will you tell me how fast light travels?
ERIC: The same way slow light travels.

TEACHER: Do you realize that light travels at the rate of 186,000 miles per second?
GWEN: Sure, it's downhill all the way.

TEACHER: Which is faster, hot or cold?
HAL: Hot. You can always catch cold.

TEACHER SAYS

Say each sentence three times quickly:

- Three shy thrushes.

- Thick thinkers tinker.

- Free thugs set
  free thugs free.

ZOOLOGY QUIZ

1. Why do lions eat raw meat?
2. How do chimpanzees communicate?
3. Why do polar bears have fur?
4. How are elephants and hippopotamuses alike?
5. Why do elephants have trunks?
6. Why do elephants live alone?
7. What can a bird do that a man cannot do?
8. What animals spend most of the day in the principal's office?
9. How do you keep an angry rhinoceros from charging?
10. How do you fix a broken ape?

Answers on next page.

TEACHER: To which family does the lion belong?

GREGORY: I don't know, teacher. No family in our neighborhood owns one.

How do scientists count atoms?

They atom (add them) up.

What do atomic scientists do when they have time off?

They go fission (fishin').

LEWIS: It's a good thing it was adults who split the atom.

ELVIS: Why?

LEWIS: Well, if one of us kids did it, they'd make us put it back together again.

ZOOLOGY QUIZ ANSWERS

1. Because they don't know how to cook.
2. They speak Chimpaneese.
3. They'd look funny in plastic raincoats.
4. Neither can play tennis.
5. They'd have trouble carrying suitcases.
6. Because two's a crowd.
7. Take a bath in a saucer.
8. Cheetahs.
9. Take away his credit cards.
10. With a monkey wrench.

What did the plant do in the computer room?

It grew square roots.

TEACHER (*to unruly class*): This afternoon, I want to tell you about the hippopotamus. Please pay attention, all of you! If you don't look at me, you'll never know what a hippopotamus is like!

ASTRONAUT QUIZ

1. Where do astronauts leave their spaceships?
2. How do astronauts feel the day after they return to earth?
3. What can astronauts do if they run out of water?
4. How do astronauts keep clean?
5. How do lost astronauts find their way?
6. How are astronauts like football players?
7. What do you call an astronaut who is afraid of heights?
8. Why don't chickens make good astronauts?
9. What kind of pills do astronauts take?
10. Where do astronauts go swimming?
11. What is an astronaut's favorite game?
12. Why is being an astronaut such a strange job?
13. How do Martians shave?
14. What do Martians say when they want to buy a large container of soda?

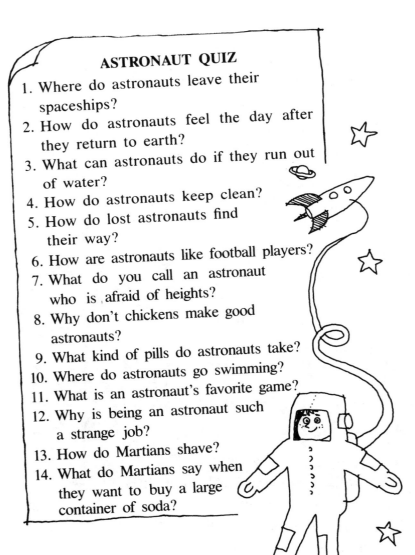

Answers on next page

TEACHER: Why did the cow jump over the moon?
MELODY: Because the farmer had cold hands.

ASTRONAUT QUIZ ANSWERS

1. At parking meteors.
2. Down and out.
3. Drink from the Big Dipper.
4. They take meteor showers.
5. They follow the Milky Way.
6. They both are interested in safe touchdowns.
7. A failure.
8. They fowl (foul) things up.
9. Space capsules.
10. In the Galax-seas (galaxies).
11. Moon-opoly.
12. Because sometimes you have to be fired before you can work.
13. With a laser (razor) blade.
14. "Take me to your liter."

TEACHER: What is zinc?

ROY: Er—where you wash your dirty dishes?

TEACHER: No, try again.

ROY: What happens when you don't know how to zwim.

TEACHER: I'm happy to be able to give you a 70 in Science.

FRED: Why don't you really enjoy yourself and give me 100?

14. BORED OF EDUCATION

TEACHER: When you yawn, you're supposed to put your hand to your mouth.
WILLY: What? And get bitten?

TEACHER: Emil, you aren't paying attention to me. Are you having trouble hearing?
EMIL: No, teacher, I'm having trouble listening.

It was a long, boring lecture, but Mary thought she had to say something nice to the teacher.
"I'd like to apologize for dozing off," she explained, "but I want you to know, I didn't miss a thing."

TEACHER: Why are you late?
CYNTHIA: Sorry, teacher, I overslept.
TEACHER: You mean, you sleep home, too?

TEACHER: Class, we will only have half a day of school this morning.
CLASS: Yippee! Hooray!
TEACHER: We will have the other half this afternoon.

Little Alice wanted to take a day off from school. She told her mother she felt feverish and achy. Her mother brought her a cup of tea and put a thermometer in her mouth.

As soon as her mother left the room, Little Alice dipped the thermometer in the tea. When her mother returned and read the thermometer, she told Little Alice to get dressed and go to school.

"But my fever is so high!" gasped Little Alice.

"You're right, dear," her mother agreed. "It's way up to 140. That means you're dead. So you might as well go to school."

GLADYS: I can't go to school today.
MOTHER: Why not?
GLADYS: I don't feel well.
MOTHER: Where don't you feel well?
GLADYS: In school.

TEACHER: That's quite a cough you have, Michael. What are you taking for it?
MICHAEL: I don't know, teacher. What will you give me?

TEACHER: You missed school yesterday, didn't you?
ROD: Not very much.

FATHER: I hear you played hookey from school to play baseball.
JUNIOR: No, Dad, and I have the fish to prove it.

VOICE (*on telephone*): My son has a bad cold and won't be able to attend school today.

ASSISTANT PRINCIPAL: Who is this?

VOICE: This is my father speaking.

A WORD

TO THE WISE GUY

Playing hookey from school is like a credit card—fun now, pay later.

Laugh and the class laughs with you, but you stay after school alone.

Some people drink at the fountain of knowledge—some just gargle.

"The brain is a wonderful thing."

"Why do you say that?"

"Because it starts working the minute you get up in the morning and never stops until you're called on in class."

KELLY: I didn't do my homework because I lost my memory.

TEACHER: How long has this been going on?

KELLY: How long has what been going on?

TEACHER'S COMMENTS ON YOUR COMPOSITION

You have nothing to say, but that doesn't stop you from saying it.

Some people can write on any subject. You don't need a subject.

Your ideas are so corny, you should dish them up with butter and salt.

I've heard brighter ideas from my parrot.

FATHER: When I was your age, I thought nothing about walking 10 miles to school.

JUNIOR: I agree, Dad. I don't think much of it myself.

"How do you like going to school?" asked Billy's aunt.

"I like the going fine," said Billy. "I also enjoy the coming home. But I don't care much for the time in between."

TEACHER: Now, Terry, be sure you go straight home.

TERRY: I can't, teacher.

TEACHER: Why not?

TERRY: Because I live around the corner.

The teacher was annoyed with her students, who kept checking the clock on the wall. She covered it with a sign that read, "Time will pass. Will you?"

When the teacher came into the classroom, she noticed a girl sitting with her feet in the aisle and chewing gum.

"Eloise," she said, "take that gum out of your mouth and put your feet in this instant!"

Knock-knock.
Who's there?
Ike, Anne, Howard, Lee, Wyatt, Tillie.
Ike, Anne, Howard, Lee, Wyatt, Tillie who?
Ike, Anne, Howard, Lee, Wyatt, Tillie (I can hardly wait till) it's three o'clock!

HOMEWORK

I love to do my homework,
It makes me feel so good.
I love to do exactly
As my teacher says I should.

I love to do my homework,
I never miss a day.
I love the little men in white
Who're taking me away.

TEACHER: Henry, I'd like to go through one whole day without having to scold you!

HENRY: You have my permission.

MY TEACHER

My teacher loves me,
Thinks I'm dear.
She's kept me for
The fourth straight year.

TEACHER: Alfred, why don't you answer me?

ALFRED: I did, teacher. I shook my head.

TEACHER: You don't expect me to hear it rattle from up here, do you?

FLO: Our teacher talks to herself. Does yours?

JOE: Yes, but she doesn't realize it. She thinks we're listening.

That last joke about the teacher was so bad, we put it at the end of this book.

Did you hear my last joke?
I sure hope so!

Index

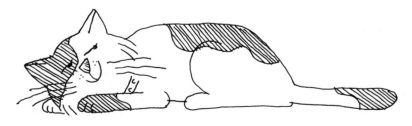